DONOR SIBLING = DIBLING

Copyright © 2020 Educate Through Nate
'WHEN A DIBLING IS BORN'
ISBN: 978-988-74044-5-3 (paperback)
ISBN: 978-988-74045-2-1 (eBook)

All Rights Reserved. No part of this book may be reproduced or used in any manner without written permission of the copright owner except for the use of quotations in a book review.
Published in Hong Kong by Melissa Jane Lavi

Copyrighted Material

Hello again, my name is Nate, and a very good day to you!

My baby dibling was born today,
a miracle come true.

He was born to Daddies' special friends,
Mummy '1' and Mummy '2'.

I still don't fully understand,
but Daddy '1' helped too.

Families with just mummies,
or just with daddies too,
need one of the other,
to make their dreams come true.

See, mummies have an egg
and daddies have a seed.

And when they join together,
a new life is conceived.

OOPS!

I'm far too young to understand
how it came to be.

I just know I have a dibling
and am as happy as can be.

We got the call this morning,
to come along and see.

This tiny little baby,
as sweet as sweet can be.

He's the cutest little baby.
10 fingers and 10 little toes.
A single curl on the top of his head
and the tiniest little nose.

My Daddies say the world is filled
with families of different kinds.
It sometimes takes a little time
to see with open minds.

Not everything is black and white,
there are many shades, they say.
That shine a different kind of light,
in an equally special way.

Just like me it started, with
a wish sent high above.
He too, was brought into this world
from a place of hope and love.

And now I must just sit and wait.
He's far too young to play.
But soon we will be best of friends,
with play dates every day.

I hope you like my story.
I have many more ahead.
Now I really have to go.
It's already time for bed.

GOOD NIGHT!

MORE IN THIS SERIES

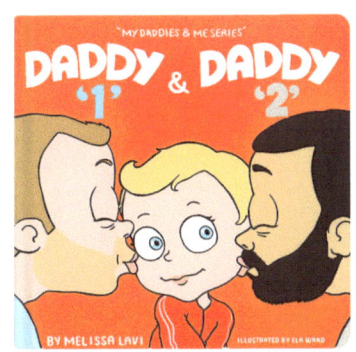

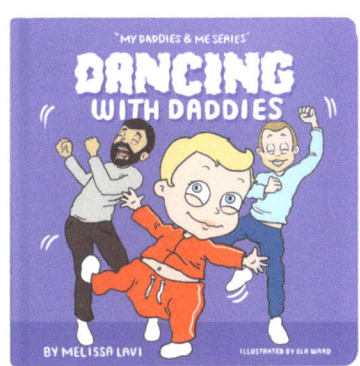

WWW.EDUCATETHROUGHNATE.COM

 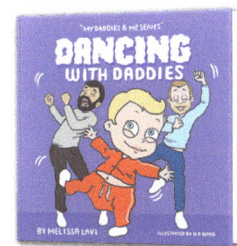 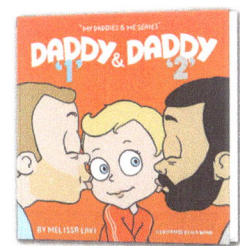   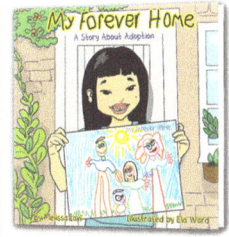
   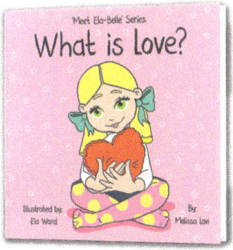 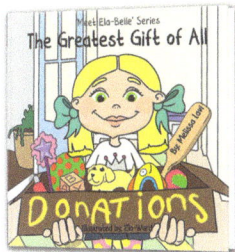 

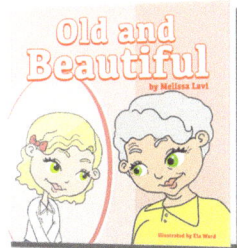

MORE FROM THIS AUTHOR AT
WWW.LOVE2READ2YOU.COM

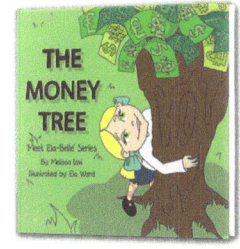